PAPER TALKS

NATIONAL
LIBRARY
OF AUSTRALIA

A catalogue record for this
book is available from the
National Library of Australia

ISBN: 978-0-6453762-3-4 (epub)
ISBN: 978-0-6453762-4-1 (paperback)

9 780645 376241

Published by Jumble Books and Publishers
(https://jumblebooksandpublishers.com)

Cover image: Brigid and Julie Morrigan

Paper Talks

by

Brigid and Julie Morrigan

Contents

Contents

Introduction (2022)

It has been a very long time since my bestie and I gathered together our Paper Talks and made a half-hearted attempt to have them published. The bulk of the original Paper Talks were thrown away at that time but the typed version with several original Talks was preserved by Brigid (aka Gillian) and kept in the envelope I sent them to her in 1988. The envelope recently came to light as Brigid was searching for some paperwork for her now grown-up son.

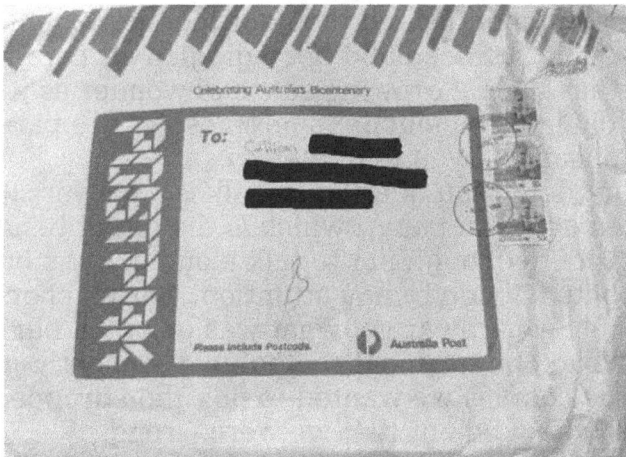

Finding the Talks again made us decide to publish them ourselves (helped by the fact that I recently started a self-publishing service so have the smarts to do this). This is the result. I will leave it to our earlier personas to speak for themselves.

Julie
January 2022

PS: We tried to adopt each other as sisters but found that isn't possible so we settled with changing our surnames and calling ourselves sisters instead.

Introduction (1988)

Paper Talks are the results of, originally, massive cases of boredom, written during classes we found less than thrilling. They were written in 1983 and 1984 in our last two years of high school as we prepared for our tertiary admissions examinations. In our last three months of high school, when the pressure was beginning to get to us, we gathered as many Talks as we could find and compiled them into a book for our own pleasure.

Since then, whenever we have been separated for several months and then got together again, the Talks have surfaced and been giggled at. Lately, there has been a growing sense of wonder as we have changed so much. Sometimes, we are barely recognisable—even to ourselves.

Our definition of a Paper Talk is a conversation written down on paper, which is the direct result of being polite enough not to talk aloud in class but not polite enough to pay attention. Our teachers probably were aware of what was going on but we never had one talk confiscated...we also both got into the courses we wanted to do...then dropped out as we found out that we were wrong...

The italicised type is Gillian's; the non-italicised is Julie's.

We hope you have as much fun reading these as we did writing them.

Julie
June 1988

PS: The rotten spelling and foul grammar are tributes to our magnificent English education. They also haven't improved with age, which is why they still remain in our conversations—both written and oral.

Paper Talk One

I have your pencil.

You sex maniac.

I think there is a mistake here somewhere.

Yes I think I agree.

I wonder where it is?

Is it in the second or first line?

Well, I think it's in the second.

I think your wrighting is terrible.

I think your spelling's bloody awful.

I hate your use of words.

You (low, inferior thing) hate my (super nice, perfect god) use of words. I sniff at you! SNIFF!

Hmmph, Hummph and Humumph.

You better watch out for the djinn.

Why?

You remember what happened to the camel?

I already have two I don't need another.

Perhaps, he'd work in reverse and make you the lopsided boob of Perth Mod.

Let's talk about something else (how did we get onto the subject of "boobs" in the first place?)

You said humph, like the camel, I warned you of the djinn, you said you had two lumps and I said he'd take one away.

That's a good summary of the conversation but, ask yourself, does that really effect the motion of the universe?

Who's talking about the universe? (sarcasm)

You were when you summarised the passage.

How?

Well 42 of course (silly goose)

I didn't mention anything about 9 x 6.

I thought you did (no referring back to the text please!)

Well, I didn't, numskull! It's all a figment of your little toe.

No, it's a pigment of your left ankle.

At least my pigment is bigger than your figment.

Does this mean we're running out of page?

No! It means we're just beginning.

lets start back at the margin.

Why?

Because it's neater.

It is not!

Well why not at the beginning of the page then?

Because you're a marginal nutcase. The wind's at the door, and absentees.

The weather's very nice today, isn't it dear.

Yes.

I thought you would have argued the point!

Why? It's a lovely day!

But, it was miserable yesterday.

We're not talking about <u>yes</u>terday.

But it <u>was</u> miserable, you have to agree to that don't you.

No! I (being me) thought (with Einstein's IQ) that it was a <u>perfectly scrumptious</u> day.

But surely you must admit that the weather was a bit miserable don't you?

NO! IT WAS LOVELY WEATHER (QUACK!)

But, don't you think it was a little biit, a teeny weeny little bit nasty?

NO! YOU FLATFOOTED BUZZARD? IT WAS GORGEOUS (GULP, SNORKEL) WEATHER.

But but but but........

SHUT UP! YOU HAIRY CORNED LARRIKIN.

NOW YOU'VE REALLY DONE IT. I HATE YOU AND
IM NOT GOING TO STHPEAK TO YOU AGEN!!!!!!
So there

LISPERS NEVER GET ANYWHERE, ESPECIALLY
WHEN THEY CAN'T SPELL! (SO SIT ON IT)

HUMM, This conversation is very interested to
analyse, don't you think doctor.

OH YES, notice how the standard of writing has
gone down the drain.

An interesting case of leptoclamia don't you agree
professor.

Definitely, with just a touch of claustrophobia.

And hydrophobia, and corns.

With a small wee bit of kleptomania.
(we're doing 5b not 4b!)

Paper Talk Two

If I said I was bored would you hate me?

If you said you was not I would!

Doesn't your grammar sound a bit faulty?

Yes but I can't really decide if it should be was or were!

It should be were, honestly, he's cute, a bit stupid, but cute.

If you think it's Boring do you want to begin a conversation?

I thought we had. I think he's on to us.

Do you? How?

He keeps glancing over in this direction and/or I have a guilty conscience (boo hoo)

He just glances in this direction because he fancies you.

Bull shit.

Yes. Perhaps he fancies me.

So modest. Main question, do you fancy him?

If his hair wasn't so curly and his body better built and his face rearranged ie someone else. Yes.

I see. He's kind of like Scruff, loveable but not in that way.

I suppose so. Scruff's more lovable though. He's just a pup, I prefere the mature type (3 years old)

I think he's over 3. I think he may be over 4.

But not in mind thought. I go for brains. Scruff's got more than him.

That's rich.

Not as rich as the teach.

Yes, I should imagine teach got paid more than Scruff.

Maybe in money but not in Pal.

I wouldn't bet on it.

I would if he hasn't got a dog.

Ask him.

He looks as if he has (That face looks like a collie)

Not a collied at all, the hairs the same fuzziness, but the shade and face are definitely a pugs.

I wouldn't be surprised if it was an English Bull terrier (Flat).

Aaah, I'd vote for pug.

What Liberal or labour.

Labour, of course, (or should it be for the national COUNTRY party, after all...)

What about the...Dare I say...Tories.

NO!

Not to mention the welsh leek (drip...drip)

We are not talking about David Lloyd George.

Who?!?!

GILLIAN ANN!!!

Welllll!

AND YOU'RE A POM TOO!

Boohoo   sniff sniff

CRYING WILL GET YOU
NOWHERE!
DO YOU HEAR (SEE?) ME?

You've used up all that space (shame on you)

You haven't answered my question (I'm supplying
the paper anyhow.)

*Yes of course I see (hear) you but that doesn't alter
the fact that I couldn't give a blind goose the
description of David Lloyd George.*

He was a welsh prime minister, whom England
<u>loved</u>!

*Bully for him. I were brought up in a wittle country
town were we farmer Folk were told nowt.*

Well goody for you.

we've run out of paper.
Would you like to share mine?

NOT REALLY.

Oh!

I THOUGHT YOU WOULD FEEL LIKE THAT!

Are you reading my mind, feelings or paper?

ALL THREE I'M OMNISCIENT.

Aren't you just marvalous.

YOU (eeugh) can't spell, (raise my nose and move it to the other side.)

I think the orange of the chairs and of the floor clash.

I think you've changed the subject.

I think we've exhausted the other.

Yes.

That's a conversation killer (just <u>yes</u>)

I know (smug pleasure)

It makes it <u>hard</u> to talk when theres not much Feedback!

I know (smug pleasure) [DON'T HIT ME]

I should jab you with a tetnas needle, then a rusty nail, then a cactus and if you survive <u>then</u> I'll hit you.

You're a maggot mixed with a faggot and then excreted by a dying sheep in the last thralls of labour.

Taa.

And then you were eaten by a mosquito carrying malaria and slapped by a hairy hand because you were eating a hairy leg and you were splattered all over the wall.

Balls.

And then you were scarped off by two mating flies.

Who were you mating with?

It wasn't me at all, it was your brother and <u>mine</u>!

AAhh now your talking sense.

You agree then.

Only the part about the sex of the flies.

You can't half agree.

No I can't, I'm only a quarter agreeing.

Alright.

And the world becomes a squashed sausage.

Yes.

Are you becoming Metaphysical of Philosophal.

What? (Your spelling is atrocious! Do you mean philosophical? If so, then I am becoming philosophical! What about you?)

I'm still normal I just can't spell, if you count a rotten speller as a Metaphysic then thats what I'm becoming.

You can't write either.

So?

Yes.

Oh.

Very.

Mmm.

Of course, I love my mummy.

So do I.

Dadada...

Shave her legs and then he was a she and she said Da dada dada da da

What, in hell, are you writing about?

Songs. I thought that's what we were talking about?

No, not precisely.

Okay forget about my last couple of statements.

I will.

What a shame that lesson's finished I was enjoying the relaxation.

Yes, have we got a double period or a single? I feel sorry for him, he looks so disappointed. It's a pity he's teaching such a dumb subject, he could wow 'em in Lit, but he's not really going to be appreciated in maths. What do you reckon?

*I recon you're right and also that is one hell of
a speech to recon with.*

You've done it again.

WHAT?

I wrote it neatly and everything (mournful).

*Well, I'll be blown if I know what you meant its to
early in the morning to judge conversations on
their previously accum'd merit.*

It's the second last period of the day, dear, in the
afternoon. And I meant your spelling, which you do
just to annoy me, you're nothing but a POM.

*(offended) Huh, I don't care if im A POM or not,
(more normal) I really have not got a head for long
words, like recon.*

If reckon is your idea of a long word, you've had it.
I mean, what about
ANTIDISESTABLISHMENTARISM?

This has me confused!

Yes, do you have any spare accounting paper you
can lend, I'm all out, but I will pay you back.

*You can have what I've got if you don't mind
splitting air.*

You've got none, then?

Yes.

Yes, we have no bananas. SIGH!!! I better go
walkabout then. Be back.

Oh, I was (or were) going to go.

Now you tell me!

I love to give people shocks.

She's used the wrong word.

Which.

Affect, instead of effect. Do I seem picky?

No.

THANK YOU.

Is that sarcastic or not.

NO. BOBBI HAS A BIG HEAD.

Yesss. She can also be a cow. I think maths is more boring than accounting don't you?

Yes. Shall we start with 25.16? No I am not hugging the book. I am just leaning my chin on it. It's very comfortable.

This means liquid paper. Her paper is yellow compared with the old stuff.

I hate to ask, but WHAT?

You know what I mean.

I get it, translation, this new paper that I went walkabouts for, is yellower than the stuff we had before, and that we need liquid paper for all the errors. Right? 25.16? TALLY-HO!

I hate to tell you this but...I've done it already.

Have I?

I don't think so, I did it on the weekend.

YOU BITCH! YOU DO IT AGAIN THEN (OR LET ME CHEAT) BECAUSE WE AREN'T BLOODY WELL TURNING OVER.

Sorry!

You're going to have to right a formal apology, while I cheat (which I'm not really doing) aren't you then? ALRIGHT!

Most honorable wonderful (forgetful Madam,
    This letter is to convey my greatest and sincerest apology for a sin which you have every right to chastise me for. I know of the seven deadly sins (as you must) but this must be the eighth and most deadly of them all.
    I respectfully request that you except my most humblist self accusation on the grounds that if I had not just had the urge to do some accounting this letter would not have been necessary.
    It would lighten my heart and clothing if you would take to me with a bull whip and then boil me in oil and then hang, draw and quarter me and then attack me in any way you see fit until you have had enough time to do 25.16 yourself.
    Most respectfully and humbly yours,
    Gillian

WAIT A TIC

Okay.

Do C.

But that would put me even further in front (But I'll do it anyway).

Don't worry.

I can't do C.

Hang on. Nice APOLOGY. DO YOU KNOW ANY SHAKESPEARE. IF SO? WRITE ON, BUT DON'T BUG ME FOR 5 MINS. (YOU COULD HAVE TOLD ME IT WAS AN I&E NOT A R&P.)

I didn't know you were doing an R&P. Funny when your asked you can never remember much Shakes.

But:—

> *If music be the food of love play on*

> *And I will halloo your name to the reverberate hills*
> *(JULIE Julie Julie Julie...)*

> *Out damn Spot*

> *Alas poor Yorric I knew him...*

> *Horatio*

> *Hello Sailor...Ship ahoy (hey wait a minute that's not Shake is it?)*

> *What light from yonder window breaks 'tis the east and Juliet is the sun.*

Nice variety. Got a thing about tragedies? Have you? C is IMPOSSIBLE.

True.

LEAVE C UNTIL WE'RE SAFE AT HOME. I DO
NOT WANT TO DO ANYTHING MORE NOW THAT
ITS PERIOD 8. BUT IF I DON'T DO IT I'LL HAVE
HOMEWORK. I KNOW...

SHE IS
    a. A VAMPIRE
    b. A GHOUL
    c. AWFUL
    d. THE PRODUCTION OF A MISMATCH
        BETWEEN TWO THINGS A GORILLA AND
        A CHIMPANZEE.

ACCOUNTING IS...
    a. BORING
    b. HARD WORK
    c. SICKENING
    d. THE RESULT OF A SYPHILIC MIND SUCH
        AS SHAKESPEARE

SHAKESPEARE WAS...
    a. A MISTAKE
    b. A PAIN
    c. A BORE
    d. A GIANT ERROR IN GOD'S JUDGEMENT
        WHICH HAS BEEN REGRETTED EVER
        SINCE.

17 MINUTES LEFT.

I HAVE STARTED 25.21.

I have stopped doing 25.21. Homework sounds
good to me, we have a test tomorrow and the TAE
IN NOVEMBER, we have no more alternatives. I'm
heartbroken, I'm bored, I'm bloody demented,
I want my mummy, I want the siren to go, I want
my desk to grow bigger, I want a new fountain pen,
I want blue hair, and pink eyes, I want
a chameleon, I want Marcelle Marceau...

It was Marcel Marceau's birthday last week.
I guess he celebrated it quietly.

I should imagine so. Does a desk look a bit
crowded. (A protozoan would have trouble finding
breathing space.)

I can't see my desk and to tell the truth I don't
want to see my desk. I have a lot of homework.
I can't find my homework. I'm having a nervous
break down (we're back to pencil)

I've noticed ALL OF THEM. I think we should start
a club.

Who's "THEM"? What sort of a club. I want
a homework sheet (I want my mummy) this place
gets to you in a way that makes you write
disjointed please for help.

That's what I mean, a club for the cancellation of
Mondays, the cancellation of accounting, the
cancellation of school, the cancellation of the years
from 16 to 17, get the drift (THEM'S ALL THE
REASON'S YOU GAVE)

I see. Did you know that if we'd've been in the
olden days (way back) we'd've been married off by
now?

Do you think it would have been better? And do you
mean in Mr B's time?

nNNo...But at least I wouldn't have such a cramped
desk.

Yes. That makes sense, do you want one lump or
two?

18

Well I like odd better than even so I'll just have 1.
How many pieces do you want?

I'd like to be complete, please.

I think elbow is a nice word. I also think windowsill
has a round sound (alliteraty) to it.

Oh! You know the reason you prefer odds, its
because you're odd, weird, I mean REALLY weird.

My pencil's blunt, the bell's about to go and we've
run out of paper (what a roundup).

Bye.

See ya later.

(PERHAPS)

lets continue tomorrow

IN A DIFFERENT CONVERSATION, I WILL HAVE
THE LAST WORD!!!

Paper Talk Three

Hello! I am beginning to be bored, we did this last year. What has he done to his hair?

I think it was washed and combed (Yech!) Can I borrow your pencil sharpener please? Taa.

What are you going to do with it?

That's a good question. Hmm...Let's see...I'll firstly sharpen my pencil (mm nice and sharp) then I'll shut him up with it and then after I've compacted it with solidified blech I'll give you it back on a plate with compliments of the chef.

Oh!

We're not starting the ck (conversation killer) again are we?

Yes!

It makes it <u>really</u> <u>hard</u> to keep a conversation going when you've got a ck sitting next to you who has <u>nothing</u> better to say then "oh" and "yes".

Is this conversation worth the bother of writing?

It depends on the altitude of the north star in conjunction with orion who crosses the southern cross!

I see, but what about the big dipper?

What has that got to do with the price of eggs on a tuesday in China especially when it's raining?

Nothing whatsoever, but we're not talking about eggs, or China, and it's not raining! But it is a Tuesday, so you got one thing right. (How did you manage that?)

It was difficult I must admit.

Should I congratulate you? Or warn you not to do it again?

It depends on your common sense (not that you have much any way) but if the world was to be blown up in twenty seconds would that give you time to give me the time to comprehend the content of your common sense.

No. My wrist has green stripes.

That's nice dear.

You must admire my tact, in changing the subject so neatly, mustn't you? (PLEASE!)

Ga-on then. How on earth could you get green stripes if you have no stuffed crocodiles? (or do you)

I DO NOT. THE ANSWER IS QUITE SIMPLE ...umm...umm...ummm... (Inspiration) YOU EAT LOTS OF GREENS! (TRIUMPH.)

That makes sense. To eat meat would you get brown ancles.

I DOUBT IT (YOU'VE SPELT ANKLES WRONG), BUT I DO KNOW THAT IF YOU EAT CARROTS, YOUR HAIR TURNS ORANGE (don't you dare!!)

Strange my hair is blond but I like carrots (do you eat lots of carrots) Scratch that

I READ THAT. YOU CAN'T GET AWAY WITH IT.
THE REASON YOUR HAIR IS WHITE IS BECAUSE
YOU'RE A PARSNIP!!

I think I'll write to "Jim'll fix it" and ask if I can get him to get me a chat with Anne Macaffry.

YOU'VE CHANGED THE SUBJECT!

So I still want to meet her (wouldn't you?)

No, she probably wouldn't live up to expectations.
Why did you change (quiver) the subject (sob)? Boo
hoo.

Okay then. You are a <u>radish</u>!

I LIKE RADISHES. SO DID RAPUNZEL.

Oh well—here goes.

Paper Talk Four

Do you think he'd look better upside down?

Sideways would look good...but...Yes I suppose upside down would perhaps make him look half way human.

Good Lord! I thought it might make him look halfway like a gorilla! I never thought in my wildest dreams that he'd look human.

He looks like a bobtail the right way up don't you agree? I suppose it could be impossible for such a creature to look like a gorilla even upside down and wrong way out.

Perhaps. But he could never look human. He looks like an ostrich.

Yes, that is why his name is what it is.

That is right. Let's burn everything every written by T.S. Eliot. Boy, has he got a terrible accent.

I don't think he should ever be allowed to speak.

He sounds worse than even Winston Churchill.

He sounds like a cross between Hitler, Churchill and Maggie Thatcher.

MAGGIE THATCHER!?! (Shriek?)

Yes. The accent that sounds pathetic is her.

I thought that that was just posh, snobby English.

Humm.

Ck.

Look whos talking.

I'm not talking. I'm not saying a word. I'm writing,
so sit on it! SO THERE!

*That makes sense. Hey, what do you say to pulling
his tonsils out through his nose?*

Good idea! Up the revolution!

Up his and all people that like this rubbish.

Yes, I agree. Kill all Poms, who aren't Lancashiran.

What spelling. That seems like a likely statement.

Well, it makes a change.

Yes you usually spout some pathetic things.

What?

*Well you have written some pathetic things in your
time haven't you?*

On occasion, but what on earth do you mean,
I can't read your writing or I don't believe it if I do.

*My writing must be really bad if even you can't
read it.*

I do believe that that was an insult.

Whom to?

Moi. (Perfection itself) How dare you? You <u>thing</u>
whom can't even spell.

Oh must humble apologies to the perfect being.

Perfect being? Do you mean me? You flatter me, indeed, you do (if I had a fan, it'd be fluttering)

I think this rendition of his poem is even worse then the one ◄— he did.

Yes, he sounds like a pug who has been strangled, buried for three months, dug up, revived and taught to speak. Do you agree?

Yes he also makes the poem twice as long as what it already is. I think he should be drawn quartered hung boiled in oil and fed to a hundred hungry fuzzy blue things.

Definitely, and then the fuzzy blue things should be destroyed and gathered together to make a fuzzy blue jumper, which should then be washed in icy water, beaten on rocks, bleached, burnt and then scrubbed in boiling water and then stuck on a briar bush to dry.

Quite right. Then they should be dismantled and baked into a pie fed to a cyclops 20cm tall and then he should be thrown off a cliff to be splattered onto a slab of slate.

And then he should be eaten by five protozoa, who split into ten, and then twenty, and then forty, and then eighty, and then one hundred and sixty...

And then?

And then the protozoa will take over the world...

Yes.

AND ALL BECAUSE OF T.S. ELIOT!!

The "Waste Land" should have been collapsed into a little ball of waste paper and shoveled up his NOSE!

From the picture, it was big enough to fit easily.

Eliots nose reminds me of his nose.

There is a similarity.

His hair style is the same, his eyebrows are the same, his hair style is the same and his neck is the same. His eyes and lips are different.

You don't like him?

Who Eliot or Him?

Both.

Oh they're okay but they look like goannas (no insult to the goanna)

Bobtail or otherwise?

Yep. The world is a green bubble.

I'd prefer purple.

Okay a purple bubble on the outside, a green bubble on the inside.

With no yellow.

Difinately Not!

I'm so glad we agree on that, some blue would be nice.

Some fluffy blue bits bouncing over the surface of bubbles. And a little blue bubble orbiting.

Yes. Sounds good, the colour scheme might be a wee bit gaudy, don't you think so.

It all depends on if its pastle or bright or smooth or rough.

You've spelt pastel wrong.

You should be an English teacher.

I think I've been insulted again.

Nah. I just think...or do I.

You do not.

I Love your subtleness and your mildness and freeness of spirit.

Thank you. It's all true.

Oh my I think this convo is getting very high faluting. Shall we come back down to the little purple green and blue bubblles or have we surpassed that primitive stage.

We've surpassed the primitive stage, he just shut her up brilliantly.

She deserves it. She can't take it though. How shallow (snobbishly said)

True. I did too.

She's fiddling with the bow on my shoe. It feels funny.

She's weird.

Yep diffinatly.

Definitely. No comment on anything as basic as spelling.

Whats rong with my spelling.

Nothing much.

Oh I <u>love</u> your way of putting things.

I thought you'd be impressed.

the words of a master.

No comment.

Oh deary me. What will she think of next.

A new sheet of paper.

Yes and a new train (choo choo) of thought.

Yes and a new topic.

Yes and some different line of conversation.

This is exceedingly boring, he sounds like he needs to blow his nose.

He probably does. I can just imagine him as an old man, his hair thin, his face and nose bloodshot, his eyes puffy and his nose extreemly large from blowing it. His body <u>bloted</u> from food and drink.

Spelling.

Bloated. What do you think of my description. Does it fit the tape (it echoes. He must be doing it in an open room).

Yes, too both. McCaverty. Depravity. Definitely Sir.

Hmm. That makes a weird kind of sense.

Paper Talk Five

"In the room
The women come and go
Talking of Michelangelo"

Well I never.

My wrist hurts. What did you never? Don't you like
my opening gambit? It's the one thing from
T.S. Eliot that I like. I thought it fitted in with our
previous topic. You VANDAL!

I'm so sorry (for both wrists and vandalism)

*I'm not quite sure if I could understand your love of
such a statement (I think you're weird).*

I didn't say that I loved it...just that I like it, if I'm
weird you're weirder.

How? You're the one who <u>likes</u> T.S. Eliot.

I SAID? AN' I REPEAT, THAT IT WAS THE <u>ONE</u>
THING OF HIS I LIKED. THE ONE PHRASE, ITS
CATCHY, IT WOULD MAKE A GREAT
ADVERTISING SLOGAN.

*What for Panty hose? I saw an advert (Dandruff)
which reminds me of that.*

I've seen it too, but its never made me think of that
it's just made me feel bilious. (isn't that a nice word
bilious, have I spelt it right do you know?)

*I know what you mean. I thought she was the
ugliest woman I have ever seen (up close) and to
think, she is supposed to be a model.*

Models are normally ugly, have you seen the new Jeans West error?

No, what is it?

It is the correct term, she is awful, I mean hair-on-end, Frankenstein's beautiful, awful. Uuugh!!

AAhh. this means the ad disagreed with your bile duct then?

Something like that. It also disagreed with my hair, it used to be dead straight, but now look at it! But then all Jeans West ads do that I mean.

Well, if you watched an ad of the opposite thing, ie food ads, it would go straight again?

I did, it went reddish.

Oh, what a shame, what are you going to do now?

I've tried everything! I'm just going to have to leave it the way it is. What happened to you?

What do you mean, Im perfect (modesty)

I mean, the shade of your hair, it wasn't always that way, was it? (INSULT) You perfect, pull the other leg it plays jingle bells.

Jingle Bells. Jingle bells all the way.

I like that song.

My hair was more red when I was younger but I didn't like it so I changed it (insult, insult, insult).

(Slog, bang, slap, plop) Your brains just fell out on the floor, because I hit you—and not too hard either (insult)

I'm so sorry you can't have your brains knocked out by me 'cause (yes you guessed it) you have none. My hand bounces off.

How could your hand move to hit me? YOUR BRAINS ARE ON THE FLOOR! (FOOL!!)

Oh I <u>love</u>...just <u>love</u>...your comment.

OH SIT ON THEM.

I sometimes think that your comments are a little weird and strange.

Paper Talk Six

I want to do a Venn diagram.

Never mind dear, you'll survive.

It is Maths.

So what, you can do biology in maths if you're so inclined.

But I want to do a VENN DIAGRAM, I never <u>want</u> to do biology, is he making sense, I can't tell.

Yes but its impossible when your dealing with this topic. (So you can't do a Venn diagram if you wanted to)

Sob, boo hoo, sniff, sniffle, snifflet, drip, drip, drip, gasp, sob, boo hoo...

If your going to be like that why not do one like this:—
>   *S has 15 members*
>   *B has 23 members*
>   *S & B share 3 members*
>   *S & B & H share 1 member*
>   *S & S share 11 members*
>   *How many has H got.*

NO. I'M GOING TO DO A PIE GRAPH, I AM ALLOWED TO DO THAT IN THIS CLASS.

Bloody fussy creature. I try to accomodate your needs and then you (little swine) go and change your MIND. HuMMPH!!!

At least I have a mind to change!!

I wouldn't be too sure of that if I were you.

How can you be sure of anything, you brainless goink? Mr B just walked in! He's on the prowl.

How dare you say that you little bleep. He's left now.

He left ages ago, you just took your time answering, I've finished my bar graph and I dare because I want to.

Your BAR Graph?

Huh?

Your Bar GRAPH?

Oh! No!

Oh Pooooo!

I'm doing it! How come you always do everything the hard way?

I don't know I'm just not working properly that's all.

Do you ever work properly.

No, (what did you expect A miracle?)

Not really, I was just curious, remiss is a nice word.

Yes very remiss of you for not muntioning it before.

Yes, but really it is a NICE word.

Nice is a nice word too.

You're batty (another nice word).

*Batty's a nice word, You're is a nice word,
another's a nice word and word's a nice word (your
turn).*

Change the subject.

Why I like nice words.

That is not a subject change. <u>This</u> is a subject
change.

What's the difference between "that" and "this"?

this has is and that has at.

*True, very true, and quite logical. (What am
I saying, I'm going batty).*

I've already said that, you fruit cake.

I must taste good.

No comment.

Paper Talk Seven

I have a question to ask.

Ask away.

Why do we have to have a double subject first thing in the morning? And worse than that, why do we have to copy down notes at the very beginning when we're not awake yet? (Snore)

It is one of the mysteries of the universe, my child, along with the 5 000 000 000, which makes for a very long explanation. The main reason being that SOMEONE in a high place does not like happy and innocent people and that you never wake up anyway. My child, think on it, life is meant to be easy, especially in relationship to Thursday mornings, which should be banned until 1.00 pm. This explanation may sound vague, my child, because it is.

Ah, wise woman of the east, if I were up to it I would ask you the answer and question to Life, the Universe and Everything, but since the answer is forty two and the question is 6 x 9, I really don't think I'm up to it right now.

My child, your infinite stupidity appalls me. The question is how many squids can you fit into an interstate phone line and the answer is 43.

Why, oh wise woman, how can this be so if Life, the Universe and Everything is 42 and your comment has the answer of 43?

My child, a long time ago my friend, Deep Thought, had a short circuit and read his own notes wrong. My child, he read 43 as 42. An understandable error, my child, as he was only a computer. You must forgive him, for leading you on.

I see wise woman. I think I can understand in my small mind a small part of your infinitely emense explanation.

I am glad, my child, it would grieve my greatness to see your miniscule mind bewildered.

Ah wise woman how wise you are.

I know, my child, I know.

Thank you for giving your time to one not worthy of your precious medatiating time and the taxing of your mind. Permit me to leave you now to seek my fortune, this information will allow me to succeed in the trials of the world.

Yes, my child, may the snurklesings of fortune go with you. Blessings.

I think the people in this conversation are ga ga foolish and absolutely insane.

You started it, my child.

I only asked a question, I didn't start with the wise cracks.

Who was wise-cracking? (SHOCK AND INDIGNATION). I was being perfectly serious. Perfectly.

Well at least I didn't start with the "my child".

The question you asked deserved a "my child" and you saying I was a wise woman made me have to keep it up, plus being smarter than you I thought it was reasonable.

Oooo (insult taken) and I thought you were a nice person too (well I didn't really but you're okay).

THANK YOU (SMUG)

There's no use casting swine before pearls is there.

Not really, but you <u>will</u> walk in front of me.

I know, we pearls should keep to our oysters and not go walking in front of the ruffian sort.

Oh, yes. But what use is a pearl, if you don't let its beauty be admired by others?

We are reserving our beauty for one special person (sigh).

Whom, may I enquire?

I've not decided whom to pin my affection on as yet.

But haven't you got an image of the lucky (SARCASM) person?

Oh, he's the classical greek God type.

You mean big nosed, short, solid, and the pinching sort?

Oh nothing like that, he's more like the physical type (not taking any notice of sarcasm).

Physical? Oh you mean the fat's really muscle and he slaps you a lot?

Very caustic.

Well?

No.

well, what do you mean? A dream boat with wide blue eyes and curly blonde hair? Or a rustic with straight black hair and bright brown eyes?

Both.

BOTH?!?

Well. If he's a greek god he can be one one day and the other the next.

Oh! Will he speak English or just Greek?

Both, he's ambidextrous too (however you spell it).

Oh, is there anything wrong with him?

NO!

He sounds bloody awful.

That's why I haven't got him yet.

Oh.

It makes sense doesn't it?

In a way.

It makes more sense than to dream about him all the time.

I suppose so (very doubtful).

Paper Talk Eight

Amelia lacks something essential.

I just think she likes to have attention to centre around her, can't stand to be pushed out of the lime light.

That and the fact that she has no brains.

True. Let's call her "Vacuum Brain".

There's not even a vacuum in her head.

What is it then.

Nothing, just nothingness, soft misty grey nothingness, kind of like a dirty marshmallow to look at.

That sounds too nice to be in her head.

It's a very dirty thing in her head, very ugly and very awful.

That's better.

It would be a beautiful thing in a nice person.

Yes I suppose it would. What would it be like and in whom?

In Juanita its like a soft, fluffy grey could, with not a speck of harm in it, but it causes untold damage because of the things it lets drop.

Why her in particular. What makes you think of her?

Because she doesn't know what she's doing, and hurts people unwittingly.

True. What about other people? Someone like...
I can't think of any one. Do you know anyone who's
soft fluffy and baby blue inside?

Yes, she's two years old and her name is Kerrie, she'll lose the sweetness as she gets older. Why are you writing with just the refill.

I don't know. Its just for fun.

Oh, do you know anyone baby blue inside?

I don't think there is anyone over 2 years old who's
baby blue inside, maybe some could be baby blue
but not that soft. Anyone who can talk is corrupt.
Imbicials could be baby blue. they don't know
what's happening (that sounds deprressing doesn't
it).

Imbeciles are not baby blue, they're a soft, greyness because they hurt people.

I suppose you're right. When the world began all
the earth was covered in green. (did you know
that?)

I always thought it was covered by sea, waves and white crests and things.

Well it wasn't when earth showed was it. (it was
before earth was formed).

Alright. It was green, slimy and mossy.

But it was still green!

I've said that, what about it?

I was just making a comment. What about red, that came after a while, when flowers first grew.

No it didn't, it came when the sun first rose, long before the greenness. Half way through the sea.

Very poetic.

Oh shut up.

Paper Talk Nine

What is your opinion of the Lenin and Marcsist movements?

Nothing really, they're just floating around outside.
(If an elegy is a poem for a dead person what is
a poem for a live person?)

*I haven't a clue (Can I borrow your pencil
sharpener). What about pink pigs.*

That's what I mean, perhaps a sonnet or an ode?

> Ode to Pink Pigs
>
> Oh pink pigs, pink pigs, pink pigs
> Your gleaming hides
> Are like a bald man's
> Shiny pate
> Your tails
> Makes Shirley Temple's hair
> Look straight
> And I like you best
> On Sunday mornings
> When you lie on my plate
> As bacon.
>
> <u>Julie</u>

What a shame, poor little pigs. I hate you pig eater.

Don't you like bacon?

Yes but not from little pink pigs.

What colour pigs do you like it from? (Do you like
my ode?)

Green (Yes.)

43

Oh, alright then. (Do you want another one?)

About purple elephants.

Alright.

> Once there was a purple elephant
> Elephant, elephant, elephant
> Who had a short little trunk
> Trunk, trunk, trunk
> So he wanted it to stretch
> Stretch, stretch, stretch
> But it wouldn't,
> Wouldn't, couldn't, shouldn't
> And that's the end of my tail
> Tail, tail, tail
> About an elephant
> Elephant, elephant, elephant.

This is a terrible poem, it's not even funny. I am depressed.

I like the bit where it goes

> *"But it wouldn't,*
> *Wouldn't, couldn't, shouldn't"*

Its really good, a good change from the other repititious lines. I like this poem better than the other one (I'm having trouble with my writing)

Is that unusual? Thank you, sincerely.

Im not sure if I should kick you or congratulate you.

You couldn't do both?

Mothtly I thitth and thinkth but
thometimeth I justh thits.

Do you?

You underthtood that? I didn't!

I'm used to it.

Why do I have the dithtinct feeling that I'm being
inthulted?

Yes.

Thatth not an anthwer.

Oh but yeth it ith. (two can play at that).

Oh, can they?

I suppose if they're so inclined.

Oh.

Ck.

Paper Talk Ten

He pinched our cricket pictures.

We should pinch them back. Do you think he would pinch this?

I suppose he could if he wanted to (if he was kinky). He keeps repeating himself.

Is that unusual, I'm writing over my 90 degree triangle.

That could be difficult.

It is fun, did you bring your appendix.

Yes. The little bits of your brain are falling down a well.

Why?

How am I supposed to know, its your brain, not mine, and even if I did I wouldn't tell you!

Bitch.

And I love you too.

I'm loveable.

Oh yes like my brother.

You succeeded. I mean if you wanted to insult me you just managed it. You are a...there are no words. You're indescribable.

Oh, there are no words to describe me. Oh thank you. (AAhh).

Yes there are. I've been thinking about it. 1st there insufferable.

And then there was one.

2nd there's dogmatic.

And then there were 2.

3rd there's hideous.

That's enough of that!

Have I upset it, didums?

Naah. I love being insinuatingly insulted about.

Then you enjoy my friendship, then?

Since you're like that. Yes.

That's why we get on so well, you like being insulted and I like insulting people. Do you like U.S.S.R.?

Which USSR, Red or other?

Other.

It's cute...It's relaxing and you have twenty minutes in class with no work. It takes time from the working day. What do you think?

Like it.

Definitely a normal ck from my friend.

Thank you.

I HATE YOU!

Isn't life splendid?

The world keeps spinning the birds keep singing and the school fans keep stopping (bad air conditioning).

True, but what about the buzz of the bees, and the hum of the cicadas and the nightmare of boredom, and the fun of not being here, and the vastness of the land, and the big wide, wide world?

Well what about it.

That was what I was asking you? To be or not to be, that is the question!!!!

It may be the question but I don't think...

I know you don't.

How could you interupt my train of thought. I've forgotten what I was going to say now! (pout)

You don't have a train of thought to interrupt, don't pout at me.

How (drip drip) could you (drip drip) you hurt my feeling (drip drip).

You have only one feeling? And is it that sensitive?

I'm not speaking to you anymore (so there).

Good.

Paper Talk Eleven

Hello!

He's rambling but that's probably because I don't know which question we're on (leading statement).

Come to that, I don't either.

Should we ask someone?

no, let's remain in happy ignorance.

Okay then

I thought you'd agree. It's a pity we asked.

Yes we're no longer ignorant and I'm not happy (boo hoo drip drip).

Don't worry, it's not really important. I think he's had his beard trimmed. Doesn't Linda look awful. It's hot in here or is getting to be. Whichever you prefer.

a)   *Yes*
b)   *Yes horrible*
c)   *Yes*
d)   *I prefer "got hot".*

I'm going to strip (just my jacket don't worry). Why don't you and surprise every one?

How would it surprise everyone?

You naked may be a "bit" of a surprise, (your ravishing body sitting voluptiously in the chair the heaving bosom rising and...) get the picture.

I didn't think of me being naked. I meant stripping as far as you. I get the picture. I wonder whether anything else (beside bosom) would rise?
(I sincerely doubt it!!!!!)

It depends on whats influencing it. He's got yellow fingers.

Oh. Oh. Triple oh. Subject change. Malaria makes you yellow. I wonder if he takes quinine.

Probably. I feel sorry for him, its about that time of year again, coming up to his yearly bout, isn't it?

I don't know. His hair's beginning to grow woolly again. Why does he keep putting his hand down his pants?

What?!?!

He was putting his hand down his pants a couple of minutes ago. Why?

I dunno. Its probably to air his genitles.

Back not front!!

So, he is a baboon.

Repeat that, slowly, with explanations.

S-o. H-e, i-s, a, b-a-b-o-o-n. (doesn't he look like one to you? he does to me!)

It was a subject change!! Yes he does.

What was (and what is an "it"?)

(You are.) (This is.) He's wearing a singlet under his short, how naff!!!

"Naff"?

Uncool, man.

Oh. I didn't know you were worried about your teachers coolness, how seweet!

No. I'm not. (What are you nattering about?) Naff means uncool, unmacho, poofterish!!!

So that means (by simple deduction) that you find his clothing offensive so therefore you would like him to change it and so by this we see you worry about his well being and you get this in every 200g block of Cadbury's dairy milk chocolate.

Oh! Well, sort of. I would like him to change his clothes, no I don't care about his well being and do singlets mix well with chocolate?

Probably not but we can see can't we.

How?

(a) Go up to him. (b) ask him very politely to stay still. (c) rip his singlet off him by various means (d) steal some money from him (e) go out and buy a block of chocolate (f) heat up the chocolate and singlet in a pan (g) freeze it and (h) see how it comes out.

I don't want to eat his dirty singlet mixed with overcooked chocolate. What do you mean by "various means"? Please describe!

I didn't mean to "eat" the chocolate you moron just to mix it with the singlet. We pinch his money to buy extra chocolate to eat while we're doing this recipe.

51

How do you expect me to describe "various means" in so short a time, I could go on forever but heres an example to tantalise you, unbutton his naval button, untuck his shirt, cut along the straps over his arms, pull away the cottiny material from his underarms and yank the cloth down until the little bell rings and whip it off him in one great big flourish.

Why don't you just rape him?

I'm not like that (beside I'd rather think of more ingenious ways to get to him).

To him? and Percy? (All sweet innocence.) Or is it Willy?

Who's Percy, Willy, etc?

He's a friendly little chap, get's a rise out of being friendly.

How much, $20 or more.

More definitely more, even though, sometimes he's below standard.

His Z score is negative.

Yes, I know. Why do you want to get to him, then? It CANNOT be for his body!!!

No is just because he's so absolutely nothingish (the cat μ)

You go for nothing? Not nice 6 ft 1 strapping, big nosed, big mouthed, nice browed hunks?

No.

You deviate!

Do you?

Yes!!!!!!!! etc !!!!

You conformist.

Big noses are not conformist! Neither's weird little accents! I don't think he's sexy, either! I think he may be lacking in that department. (Compartment?) I think he's cute. Sex doesn't come into it. And I like brown eyes, and straight noses!!!

That's a tall order, can he fill them all?

He's a tall person. Average height for a man is 5 ft 8 and he's 6 ft 1 that's five inches over the order.

Never mind dear you'll survive.

I wasn't complaining.

I never said you were.

I never said you did. Your comment just sounded as if you were comforting me, the way you do when someone complains.

I wasn't. What happens when someone complains?

You either tell 'em to shut up or you hit 'em or you comfort 'em!!!! I prefer hitting 'em meself.

That doesn't make sense.

(This is one scraggy piece of paper.) Yes it does, if someone complains tell 'em to shut up or hit' em or comfort 'em. I'd go for the hittin' method meself.

Oh. (faintly bemused, stunned and sleepy)

Disappointment. Which do you use?

Which what?

Which method of stopping complaints do use?

Ignoration.

Now that's new, I've never tried that. Does it work (talk to me !!!!!!!!!!!!!!!!!!!!!!!!....)

I dunno I've only tried on males at this school so I wouldn't know if it works on humans.

Oh (You talked to me! Hallelujah!!!!!! Brother!!!!!)

Oh!?

As you want to do this, I shall write a nice <u>long</u> letter and then do something else.

   To my friend Gillian,

        Groaning quietly over silly maths sums
        She sits, bravely facing
        The standard deviate
        At the front of the class room
        Her pale face flushed
        With exertion and sneezing
        Her soggy damp tissue at the ready
        In her hot clammy little hand
        Her bleary blue eyes
        Giving evidence to the excess of
        Emotion, maths raises in her

54

She slowly mutters "goo"
And then "muck" and then
She sighs and turns back
To her romantic fancies
Of probability
While the 5 ft 11 idiot
At the front
Jumps about in an ecstasy
Of joy at her seeming attention
Little knowing that beneath
That noisy exterior
There lies an even noisier person!
The siren goes
And her ears prick up in hope
She throws her maths book to the floor
And gathers lovingly her accounting
book
And cradles it to her body
And murmurs soft loving words to it
Placing it carefully on the table
She flips open her tatty file
And tries to catch the cascade
Of escaping paper
Sitting down
She gazes earnestly
At the imp in red who stands at the front
Wielding a green texta and the overhead.
She sighs, laughs, then gurgling with
pleasure
She picks up her pen and begins working
The spider crawl across the page,
That she calls writing
Covers page after page of paper
Notes scatter everywhere
As she stands up eagerly
To gather more tissues
For the perpetually running nose
She dashes to the office
And is back before you can blink
With fresh tissues

With her eyes alight
She tears through
The seemingly endless stream
Of accounting
Until, I, poor reprobate that I am,
Lead her astray
With wicked little tricks
And funny little notes
Ah me! It is my fault
That she says "excretion" instead of
"shit"
My fault
That she curses fluently in Russian
My fault
That her wrinkled little brow
Straightens in astonishment
Then crinkles with laughter
My fault, it is my fault.
I am lower than the low
Where she is higher than cowpats
I am ashamed
Ah, my friend, forgive me,
My childish follies—
But I know you will
You who are above cowpats
She smiles serenely
And frowns at her accounting.

by
me!

To the clock,

Tick the minutes away
You slow crawler
Tick 'em away
And hurry up about it!
I see you there—
High on the wall
Your snooty minute hand

Pointing up instead of down
Your bustling second hand
Going nowhere
But hurrying endlessly
Endlessly...
Slowly, slowly
The minute hand moves down
Pointing straight out the door now
Believe me, clock
I'd love to go outside!!!
The student's friend
And the teacher's enemy
Clock, sweet clock
Tick the minutes away
Until half past
And then I can go!
Hurry up!
CRAWLER! SUCKHOLE!

Prescriptions of soggy tissue
You moronic idiot,
Leave me cold
As do descriptions
Of last week's rubbish.

Paper Talk Twelve

You sound as if you're enjoying her description.

You are joking, aren't you? Please!

I was being sarcastic.

I'm so glad!!!!!!

You sounded like it when talking to her.

I'm getting good at lying...I mean being polite.

Yes. It's a pitty that type of person can't see it. (You're being as plain as day to me!)

I suppose I don't really lie effectively.

Maybe in her eye but not to me.

Ohl Ummm. I think one of just contracted the other. I don't know which.

Confusion is your speciality.

Why thank yer very much dearie.

Flatulation.

Speak ENGLISH for God's sake!

Who's?

The Prime minister's.

Oh (bemused) coagulation.

(You're BEMUSED!!) STUNNED SILENCE!

(Not just bemused but a llittle confused as well)
<u>*oxygenated*</u>

*When a pickle jumps on the back of a roaming
kangaroo he jumps around and doesn't like it so he
changes to an emu and is very happy until he gets
eaten.*

My mind is not here. It is somewhere else, don't
call it back.

Why not.

Because it's happy where it is.   ·

                                        ·
See this | that <u>was</u> you, this <u>is</u> you ⋰. Talk to
Goran, perhaps you'll get intelligent conversation,
you 🐾

*Since your brains exploded I may get some
intelligence out of you yet.*

That explosion was not my brain it was what I was
thinking of doing to you, you moron!!

Oh? I thought you weren't talking to me.

I'M NOT. I'M YELLING!!

Paper Talk Thirteen

Hello! Bell bottoms ride again!

Yep, you always start off with "hello". Why not something different, good bye, no that's not original, how about perhaps:—

Perhaps.

Maybe— I had a weird dream last night, do you want to know about it? Good. I stuck my hand in the ground outside of a house and pulled out some and then my hand came temporarily up in warts, then we went into the house through a small hole in the wall but I wouldn't 'cause there was something inside, so I made another person go first. Then it changed and were being chased all around this space aged building and kept getting caught, we were prisoners, then we got into a theatre to watch a film and I woke up.

Interesting. I don't remember my dream.

Pit it'd probably be goodish knowing you. What do you make of mine.

You have a chase complex. Otherwise, nothing much.

What about the first bit (that was the bit I didn't enjoy—I enjoyed being chased, it was a challenge to try and escape).

I don't know! What do you think I am—psychic?

Probably, possibly,—yep.

Oh. Well, I'm not!!!!!!

Oh but you are, you just don't know it.

If you want me to be, alright.

Well then tell me about my dream then.

It meant that some time in the future you are going to be searching for something you want very much, but the going will be hard and painful and in the end dangerous.

Thanks, you've really made my day.

I wonder why?

Swine.

What does that have to do with anything?

Not a lot but it just means swine.

I'm afraid I don't understand.

Good.

You are not helping this conversation.

So? We can't carry it on through accounting any way.

So sad!

You sound upset!

I'm not, believe me. I'm not.

I didn't think you would be.

Paper Talk Fourteen

~~Any stories I write are for me!~~

I'd like to talk but I couldn't find a paper.

What, right a story?

What do you mean?

I meant write a story but I spelt it wrong. I supply the paper, you supply the conversation. Isn't it a lovely day!

A beautiful day. Tom the cat came out of the barn.

Why did Tom the cat come out of the barn?

I dunno that's for you to decide.

He came out because Tina the Puss was outside.

Tina purred "hello" and Tom bowed as the gentleman he was.

Tina then saw Tony Cat and fell in love with the city slicker. Tom was heartbroken!

He went to the city sliker and bit off his head and at his display of strength she sighed to him and fell back in love with him. He smiled and bowed like the gentleman he was.

But inwardly he as disgusted at someone so fickle so he went off, searching for someone special.

She followed in his wake and followed him, until one nighty he disappeared. She looked and looked for him but could not find him until she came to end of a road and she his bright face rise above the road and she called after him and is still heard until this day calling to him in the night (isn't that cute)

The End.

P.S. And she died because a car came along and squashed her flat.

Good.

Yes. It is. Mundane even.

Not really, it could be a good explanation to account for cat's schreecking at the moon.

Yes, it could be, but I always thought it was the males that screeched and you've got a female calling after him.

So we've shed new light on it.

Oh. Oh. Oh. Why do wolves howl at the moon then?

Wolves like to eat dogs and other small animals.

Oh. Why do they howl at the moon?

'Cause the moon's a dog and they're trying to get at him, besides the cat in her dumbness told the wolves about the dog and asked them to help her and so they did only to try to eat him when he gets down.

What dog?

The dog that turned into the moon, you moron.

(You're a moron) HUH?

(You're a bigger moron) the dog turned into the moon in the story, you remember, don't you? The cat chased after it.

(You're the biggest moron) It was Tom the CAT that turned into the moon, you TWIT!!!!!

I see well they're baying at Tom the Cat then.

OH BOY!

Paper Talk Fifteen

This is a piece of provided paper. It has been provided for the exclusive use of two or more persons to have a "Paper Talk"®.

Oh. I was going to ask what the paper had been provided for but you answered it already. Pilcher ate people.

Pilcher is a piltchard.

No, he's a cannibal.

A cannibalistic piltchard.

Alright. He's going bald.

Who is, Pilcher the Piltchard?

Do you, by any chance, mean Pilcher the Pilchard?

I thought that's how you spelt it. I had it like that in the first place but changed it. I am riddled with a sense of low self esteem.

Oh dear poor Gillian, do you want to muck around but you don't know where to start?

Yes.

Is this helping you?

No.

We'll stop then.

Stop what.

Stop talking.

I'm not talking (seeing mouth is very firmly closed).

Stop writing then!

I like writing.

Oh.

That doesn't help.

Your writing's darker than mine.

So I press on harder obviously.

And messier. Your writing is messier.

So? What does that mean.

You've got a messier mind? Can you draw
a vulture? A vampire? A defunct urbanac? If so, do
so?

What's a defunct urbanac?

Andrea. She's not here. ∴ she's defunct.

Ahh I see. No I can't draw a defunct urbanac.

But a vulture? A vampire? You must try!

*A vulture has been drawn,
i.e.*

Beautiful. Now a vampire.

Okay. One vampire.

Lovely (indistinct, but lovely). Now an ogre, and an octopus.

An ogre? Okay, an ogre—a long armed short ogre

an octopus

A happy smiling octopus. Now, an emu and an elegant edifice.

Whats an edifice?

Building.

Ahhh.   *an emu*

this is an archway

I WANT A WHOLE EDIFICE.

Ahh okay

but it ain't elegant

I WANT AN ELEGANT EDIFICE! (SCREAM!)

Okay okay calm down

It's elegant alright!!!?!

Now, I want a platypus and a piglet.

I want a nicer piglet!

Fussy beggar

A NICER PIGLET!

*That's the only kind of piglet I know how to draw
you fussy creature feature.*

O.K. I'll forgive you, now an ear of corn and a cricketer.

One ear of corn swaying in the breeze.

and a cricketer.

What happened to his waist? It looks more like wheat, than corn!

Sorry about that. Its just how they turned out.

TRY AGAIN!

An ear of corn still in packing

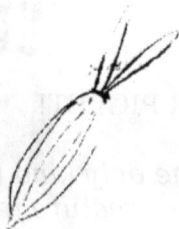

Ohhh I remember...

there you go.

AND THE CRICKETER!

Forget the cricketer.

NEVER!

I thought you couldn't.

Of course I can't! Cricketers are nice.

Grr.

DRAW IT.

No.

Please. Or at least but in a waist on the one you've drawn.

He is now a fat cricketer.

Put a waist in!

To write with... have you got a safety pin?

71

Hello Comet. Hello Pengrip.

Hello Jewely
Hello Jooly
Hello Juley
Hello Juily
Hello Gewely
Hello Gooly
Oh Golly

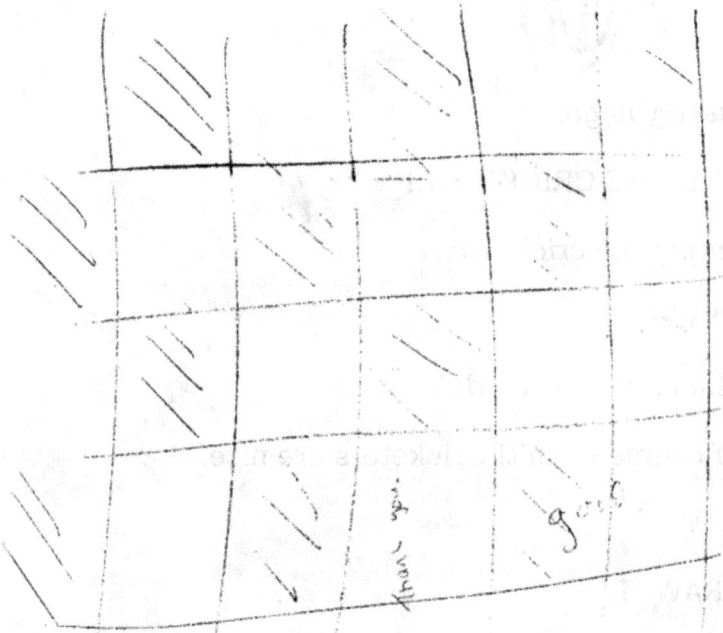

Paper Talk Sixteen

That pen you picked up's quite nice, a bit scratchy. Whose is it do you think? (SCRATCHY IS AN UNDERSTATEMENT!!!!)

What's so scratchy about it. Its just on a ruff background that's all.

There's glue all over my pencil case.

Shame

You're bloody right it is.

What'ch'y'goin' to do.

Shut the damn thing and ignore it for the rest of the period.

Oh. The weather's acting funny isn't it.

I haven't noticed it doing anything. What has it been doing.

Acting as if it were almost summer.

That's Australia for you. It's pouring in England. It'll probably rain all summer.

Probably. You forgot a question mark.

That was a long time ago!!!!!!!!!!!!!!!!!!!!!!!!!!!!!!

So you still forgot it.

It's not nice of you to mention it!!!!!!

SNIFF
SOB

BOO HOO
SOB
SNIFF

Sorry I didn't mean it (sniff) I can't stand to see someone cry (boo hoo).

Oh! Didums!!!!!! DON'T CRY (WICKED LAUGH OF JOY)

Grrrrrrrrrrrrrrrrr Grrrrrrr

Is it upset?

No (silken malice.)

Well, it's a silly didums (all sweetness).

I don't understand you! Turnips are green.

And radishes are red. (I know you don't. Isn't life wonderful?)

I wish this change of subject could be successful. All green turnips in this class are going to be distroyed (duck Julie).

Since when have I been green? A turnip? A DUCK? (DISTROYED????? What's that???)

Since day one.

What day is this?

Day 1 one eine...

You mean that Life, the Universe and Everything began this morning? That today è il giorno uno?

Yes.

Than how come I can remember last night? La sera scorsa?

How should I know maybe you dreamed it. Maybe it was an figment of your imaging, maybe we're all figments of some perverted mind.

Your mind (the one that produced you) is more than perverted, it's bloody demented!!!

So's yours.

My own mind, (my universally encompassing mind) or the mind (the very genius mind) that created me?

No, your own demented mind, pick up the book.

I have picked up the book, you mouldy, green, overripe, smelly, poisonous pickle!!!!

How can a pickle be poisonous? If it were poisonous it wouldn't be a pickle 'cause no one would have tasted it if it were poisonous would they, you pugnatious plinking piano crustacean.

Does that make sense?

Yes.

Where? You brainless aardvark!! (That is an insult on your nose!!)

Is it?

75

YES!! But then again maybe not.

Good.

It definitely is!

Oh.

K.U.

CK. I hate you.

PBS.

Oh.

THE PICKLERS BLOOD SOURCE.

Presbitarian Bludgers scourge.

SOUNDS GOOD

Priceless Buffet Sausage.

Pricks Booty Snobs.

Punky Billiard Soup.

An Original Page from Paper Talk Eleven

Julie starts this conversation with "Hello!" and then Gillian responds.

Hello!

he's rambling but that's probably because I don't know
which question we're on (leading statement).

Come to that, I don't either.

Should we ask someone?

no, let's remain in happy ignorance.

okay then

I thought you'd agree. It's a pity we asked.

yes we're no longer ignorant and I'm not happy
(boo hoo 's day trip)

don't worry, it's not really important. I think he's had his
beard trimmed. Doesn't Linda look awful. It's hot in
here or is getting to be. Whichever you prefer.

a) Yes
b) Yes horrible
c) Yes
d) I prefer 'got hot'.

I'm going to strip (just my jacket don't worry)
why don't you and surprise everyone.

How would it surprise everyone?

You naked may be a bit of a surprise, (your
twisting body sitting voluptuously in the chair
the heaving bosom rising and ...) get the picture

I didn't think of me being naked. I meant stripping
as far as you. I get the picture. I wonder
whether anything else (beside bosom) would rise? (I
sincerely doubt it!!!!)

It depends on what's influencing it. He's got yellow
fingers

Oh. Oh. Triple de subject change. Malaria makes you
yellow. I wonder if he takes quinine.

77

9 780645 376241